Gestalt Practice:

:Dick Price

Gestalt Practice::Dick Price

by John Francis Callahan for The Gestal Legacy Project

Copyright © 2019

ISBN: 978-0-359-35358-3

Dick Price never published anything about Gestalt during his lifetime. However, it is possible to reconstruct many of his ideas from talks he gave to groups at Esalen Institute. This book is an adaptation of Dick's ideas about Gestalt Practice. It is based upon his own words with only minor modifications to create the narrative form of the text. The intention is to assemble a conversational presentation – as if Dick were talking about his practice to a training group in a meeting room at Esalen.

There are several good books about Gestalt Practice that have become available in the past few years, like the "Manual of Gestalt Practice in the Tradition of Dick Price" and "The Life and Practice of Richard Price." This slender volume is designed to add a first-person introduction to that growing body of literature about Dick's work.

--John Francis Callahan, 2019

Tao Te Ching
11.

Thirty spokes support a wheel, but it is
the hole at the center that allows the
wheel to turn.
It is not the clay the potter throws that
gives the pot its usefulness, but the empty
space inside.
Without a door the room cannot be
entered, and without a window the room
is dark.
Such is the utility of emptiness.

To start off this morning I want to say something about my own background, as a way of explaining how I came to develop my approach to Gestalt.

I was born in Chicago in 1930. My parents were very affluent people because my father was a successful corporate executive. I suppose you could say that my parents, socially, were pretty much normal Americans for that time, which actually might have been the source of a lot of the difficulties we had in our relationships.

I graduated from high school in 1948. And I decided that I wanted to go to Stanford University because Stanford's relative informality appealed to me and I probably wanted to get as far away from my family as possible. Leaving home felt like a liberating escape from my mother's controlling attitude and it got me away from my father who I regarded as absent and withdrawn into his business life.

I began my college career studying economics, which I guess was kind of an Oedipal attempt to become a successful businessman like my father. Economics turned out to be a subject that did not have a lot of interest for me. An introductory psychology course did spark my interest and I changed my major to psychology. I became a serious student and maintained a 4.0 grade point average. I also developed a new career plan – one I hoped could extricate me from the status-seeking type of life I associated with my parents. My plan was to go to graduate school in psychology, become a psychologist, and eventually work as a professor or psychoanalyst. At Stanford I became a student of Gregory Bateson who was sort of an anthropological psychologist of relationships and who went on to develop the double-bind theory of schizophrenia. In fact, Bateson eventually became a big supporter of Esalen Institute.

Anyway, I earned my B.A. in Psychology from Stanford in 1952 and applied to Harvard University's newly created graduate program in social relations. I began work at Harvard that fall. I wasn't interested in being an experimental psychologist. I was interested in, you know, if I had to label it in any way, in being a kind of anthropologist of mental health and illness, and social relations seemed to be a department where this might be possible to pursue.

Harvard proved to be a huge disappointment for me. I had the naïve hope that the department of social relations would be more socially enlightened and less hierarchical than Stanford's psychology department with its focus on experimental psychology, rats, and questionnaires. Instead, the initial course of study at Harvard directly focused on experimental psychology. I also found the department to be hierarchical, authoritarian, and filled with academic bickering. Toward the end of my first year, I wrote an examination that used the material I was learning to criticize what the department was doing. As a result, I got a "C," which was really bad grade. Henry Murray, who was a famous psychologist at that time, was the only professor in the department who showed any interest in helping me.

So in the summer of 1953, I decided to leave Harvard. I told my parents I was going to transfer to either Stanford or the University of California at Berkeley. In the fall, I registered for some courses at UC Berkeley, including a course taught by Carl Rogers, the well-know humanistic psychotherapist who was a visiting psychology professor at Berkeley.

I was feeling somewhat adrift, so I decided to join the Air Force and take advantage of opportunities that seemed to exist in the armed forces for psychology majors. But instead of working in the field of psychology as I hoped, I was given a job doing obsolete gunnery research. It soon became clear to me that the Air Force was a little like Harvard, and I didn't get along too well with the people who were running it.

I was able to get a transfer to Parks Air Force Base in Pleasanton, California, where I took a position as a teacher of recruits. It was good duty. My schedule was two days on – night duty for twelve to fourteen hours – followed by two days off. That meant I could go back to school. Both UC Berkeley and Stanford were only a half-hour's drive from Pleasanton.

In the spring of 1955, I started taking courses again at Stanford. One of the courses was taught by Frederic

Spiegelberg who was a popular professor at Stanford, and who was teaching a course on the Bhagavad Gita. For the first time, I began thinking there was something in religion; it was more than a system of deceit and enforcement of social rules. At Spiegelberg's suggestion, I went to the Vedanata Society in San Francisco for a lecture. I was impressed. Spiegelberg also recommended Alan Watts' lectures to his students. I went and was immensely impressed; it was like nothing I'd ever touched into. Alan Watts was on a weird trajectory from England. He was recently resigned as an Episcopalian priest in Chicago and had turned into a San Francisco Zen Guru. Watts profoundly affected me and I began taking courses at the Academy of Asian Studies where Watts was principal teacher. He was working at the time on his influential book – Psychotherapy East and West.

I took a room at the Academy and spent even more time in San Francisco studying Buddhism, meditation, and observing the new Beatnik scene that Watts was linked up with. Beat luminaries, like Gary Snyder, Jack Kerouac, Allen Ginsberg, and Lawrence Ferlinghetti, all attended Watts' lectures.

I also began to hang out at The Place – a North Beach nightspot on upper Grant Avenue where I could get a pitcher of beer and find somebody interesting to talk to. At that time, I developed acquaintances with both Snyder and Ginsberg.

Experiences that I was having with meditation practice were feeding into new feelings of expansiveness. At the Asian

Academy I studied the writing of Nyanaponika Thera, a German-born Buddhist Vipassana meditation teacher, and his book – The Heart of Buddhist Meditation. I began having some intense spiritual experiences, some of which excited me and some that were disconcerting. I needed some guidance so I went to my teachers at the Asian Academy. Unfortunately, the knowledge of teachers at the Academy was more intellectual than experiential. They couldn't help me. I felt that the only people who could really relate to my actual experience were people involved in the Beat scene, like Gary Snyder.

Gary took me for a hike in Marin County, north of the Golden Gate, up around Mt. Tamalpais. I suppose that was an introduction to hiking as a way of managing my excitement, and it was something that stayed with me here in Big Sur as I explored the Santa Lucia Mountains behind Esalen.

Anyway, after that hike, back in San Francisco a few months later – it was December 1955. A Beat friend of mine named Gia-fu Feng came by the Academy to have dinner. Gia-fu was born in China but went to the Wharton School of Business in Philadelphia and then came to San Francisco as a teacher of T'ai Chi Chuan. Gia-fu introduce me to a woman he brought along to dinner. Her name was Bonita Fabbri, but everybody called her "Bonnie." She was a very beautiful Italian dancer who had grown up in Chicago. Bonnie was friends with Marilyn Arnold who was one of Gary Synder's sweethearts. We all called Marilyn by the name "Neuri." At the time, I was toying with the idea of becoming a Buddhist monk. So thoughts of a long-term relationship or marriage were a long way from my mind. But one thing led to another and after a couple of months I married Bonnie. We were married at the Soto Zen Temple in San Francisco, in a ceremony performed by a Zen monk, in February 1956. My parents, to say the least, were not very happy with the wedding. I had to admit to myself that part of myself was probably trying to shock my parents. My experience was very much like....*Hey, you know there's this other me that's somehow vaster and greater, and then there is the other Dick up at the altar being married by a Zen monk.*

After my parents left for Chicago, Bonnie and I moved into an apartment in San Francisco. I split my time between Bonnie, my job at the Air Force base, the Asian Academy, and the North Beach Beat scene. The high-energy state I was in made all of that possible. I was getting by on just two hours sleep a night.

So I was experiencing an upwelling of energy that I was barely able to contain. At the time, especially with Bonnie catalyzing this, I started to go crazier and crazier with activity. But in a way, for me it was just this immense expansion and excitement which I was having trouble containing.

On one of my visits to North Beach, the huge state of internal energy I was riding burst through. I was in a bar with some Beat friends. I felt a tremendous opening-up inside myself, like a fiery dawn. The bar had a fireplace. In the state I was in I thought it would be a great idea to light a fire in celebration of this mysterious event. I danced around the bar, chanting: *"Light the fire."* ... *"Light the fire."* Instead of lighting a fire, the bartender called the cops and six large San Francisco policemen handcuffed me and wrestled me into a prisoner van.

After an initial detention I was transferred to the hospital at Parks Air Force Base where I was stationed. At Parks I was given a couple of electroshock treatments and an occasional dose of Thorazine to calm me down, but in general I appreciated the caring way I was treated. For three months I was going through all sorts of experiences, some of which I remembered, some of which I didn't. One was a regression through history in which I felt like I was leaping through a series of past lives. Of particular importance was when the regression of lives came to an end – coming to a life that was some type of monk who spent his time in meditation. While in the hospital I had what could be understood from a Zen perspective as a "satori" – or an enlightenment experience.

After about three months at the military hospital, there was a major shift in my experience. I was in a balanced, fine energetic space and I remember my feeling was one of gratitude – to the nature of things and to my own nature. I was still a little volatile but I was no longer in the super excited state. Instead, I was in kind of a balanced state – a state that in some way I felt washed clean.

I had come through an experience that Gregory Bateson would later call a "transitional psychosis" and I was ready to get back to my old life and marriage. The Air Force was planning to release me from the hospital and give me an honorable discharge so I could go back to school, despite the fact that I had another year and a half of my enlistment to serve. My preference was to get out as soon as I could. I wanted to stay on the West Coast. I didn't want to go back into my old family situation.

The discharge from the hospital at Parks Air Force Base never came through. Instead I was notified that I was being transferred to another hospital. My father had arraigned for a transfer to an Air Force hospital in Illinois located about fifteen miles from the family home. My parents moved Bonnie back into their house in Chicago. But things did not go well between Bonnie and my mother. And then there was a whole series of duplicitous events perpetrated by my parents that resulted in my involuntary commitment to the Institute for Living in Connecticut.

My parents demanded that I try a course of treatment at this famous mental hospital. So to mollify them I voluntarily entered the Institute for Living in Connecticut on December 7,

1956. But in order to charge my parents for the most expensive kinds of treatment, the psychiatrists at the hospital labeled me with a bogus diagnosis of paranoid schizophrenia, and my father had me committed. As soon as I was legally committed, my parents had my marriage to Bonita annulled.

Over the next nine months I received fifty-nine insulin shock treatments, ten electroshock treatments and large doses of Thorazine. The Institute for Living was little more than a private prison in which I was being tortured. I seriously feared for my life.

I decided I had to escape. But I knew that in my weakened condition I simply was not capable of climbing over the hospital wall. I needed to get myself into better condition, despite what they were doing to me. To begin with, I learned to "cheek" the Thorazine pills they were giving me, rather than swallow them. But the electroshock treatments were taking a big physical and mental toll. The insulin shock treatments were the worst. They would knock me out and I would wake up, unable to move. When I could move again, I would continuously walk the hospital halls, drinking large amounts of water. My weight ballooned from 145 pounds to 240. I began to wonder how many more treatments it would take to kill me. I thought I'd come very close to dying a couple of times already.

Feeling desperate, I made up my mind that escape was my only option. They would not let me exercise in the hospital.

But I did my best to get into better shape, anyway, and I finally lost enough weight to make it over the wall.

It was August of 1957. I was dazed. I was an overweight young man in a hospital uniform walking around on the streets of Hartford, Connecticut. I must have looked pathetic. I had just climbed over a wall in order to escape from the most expensive mental hospital in the United States. As I walked down the street in Hartford a single thought repeated itself over and over in my mind: *Now what?* I realized that I really did not have an answer.

The first person who seemed to notice me was a bum sitting on the curb at a street corner under a tree. I sat down next to him. I decided I could trust this bum and told him all about my family and how they had tricked me into the mental hospital, how they had me committed then had my marriage annulled. Eventually we talked about what I should do next. I came to the realization that I was still too weak to make good my escape. I realized that the only way out of this horrible situation was to go back into the hospital.

The bum gave me some change to call my father from a pay phone. I made the call and told my father I had escaped but could not make it in the world right then. I said to my father, *"They've made me so ill, I literally have to recover my health. I'm not well enough to come out into a job or anything. I'm not even asking for you to get me out, now. I can't stay out, I may have escaped but I can't just go out there. I'm sick, now. I'm going to go back but I want you to get me on an open ward so I can regain my health."*

Fortunately, my father did what I asked. He told me to go ahead and return to the hospital. He had me placed on an open ward. My treatment was discontinued. And I began the long process of recovery.

Three months later, on Thanksgiving Day 1957, I was release from the hospital after a stay that lasted just short of a year. I was still weak. So I moved back in with my parents and took a job in the Chicago sign business that was run by my uncle Louis. I worked as an assistant purchasing agent.

In the aftermath of my ordeal, I spent a lot of time thinking about my experience in the mental hospital. I realized that there was a fundamental mistake being made, and the mistake was supposing that the healing process I was going through was a disease, rather than the process whereby the disease could be healed. The disease, if any, was the state prior to the so-called psychosis. In fact, the so-called psychosis was an attempt toward spontaneous healing. It was a movement towards health, not a movement towards disease. In some categories of understanding it would be called a mystical healing – really, a re-owning and discovery of parts of myself.

In any event, working for my uncle in Chicago was dull, but it allowed me to get my feet back on the ground. After three long years of working for my uncle, I found out that my old Beat friend, Gia-fu Feng and some other friends were starting a cooperative living arrangement in San Francisco. It was called the East/West House. I decided it was time to go back to California and restart a life. My parents did not try to stop me. In May of 1960, I got onboard a 707 jet airliner in Chicago that was headed for California. My intention was to make a place where people who were going through the type of bad experience I had, could simply get better treatment, and to utilize whatever I might find, to do that, back out in California.

In San Francisco, I made a connection with another Stanford graduate – Michael Murphy. We had not known each other at Stanford, but we ended up living next door to each other at the Cultural Integration Fellowship, which was a meditation center on Fulton Street. We both had been influenced by the teachings of Eastern traditions and meditation practices. We both had studied with Stanford Professor Frederic Spiegelberg and Alan Watts. We both had non-standard experiences in 1956 that led to rejection of expectations of our families and society. For me it was the experience of hospitalization at the Institute for Living. For Mike, his experience was going to India for a stay in an ashram dedicated to the famous guru, Sri Aurobindo.

Mike invited me to go down to his family's property in Big Sur. Of course, it was the old hot springs resort that became

Esalen Institute. We loaded our possessions in an old Jeep pickup truck and drove down the coast from San Francisco. Our shared intention was to start some kind of center for Eastern and Western learning. In early 1962, just four years after my release from the Institute for Living, I became the co-founder with Mike of what we would later call the Esalen Institute. One of my hopes for our project was that it would eventually become the kind of place that could offer help to people who were going through difficult psychological experiences.

At the time I had been talking to a friend who was a psychiatrist, who had himself been hospitalized. He had gone into psychiatry and we talked about finding a place that would be more than the ordinary mental hospital. Michael's interest wasn't specifically in this area. He had spent over a year at that ashram in India and his interests were more contemplative and intellectual. So we had originally talked about taking over the place as a conference center that would in some way apply itself to a range of interests – meditation, religion, extraordinary experiences, whether religious or psychotic.

We took over the property in October 1961 and co-founded the actual business that would become Esalen Institute in early 1962, and we held our first seminars that same year. My Beat connections came back to help. Gia-fu Feng came down from San Francisco. He taught T'ai Chi and kept the books on his abacus. The new business started slowly. Esalen gradually gained momentum throughout the next decade.

We started with the connections we had – people like Alan Watts – and we began to set up programs. One of the first programs – probably early 1962 – was Alan Watts. Alan did his program from his own mailing list. We used people who had their own followings, their own mailing lists. We would provide the place as a conference center for them. Then Abraham Maslow, the famous humanistic psychologist, just dropped in one night, and he became a long-term supporter. Gradually, I think the following year, we put out our own catalog and formed Esalen as a separate entity. Before that we were running Big Sur Hot Springs, just running weekends. We gradually got a few five-day programs, but otherwise we were running for "drop-in traffic." Then – I think by 1967 – we took the Big Sur Hot Springs sign down and put the Esalen Institute sign up and attempted to make the whole place a conference center. The big turning point was the people who came to be in residence – primarily Fritz Perls in 1964 and Will Schutz in 1967.

So my interest in Gestalt came about as a direct result of Fritz Perls' presence at Esalen Institute. This morning you've heard me explain how it happened – how it came about that Mike and I started Esalen. That was about two years before Fritz arrived here. At first, Fritz came up from L.A., where he was working with Jim Simkin, merely to do a Gestalt program at Esalen. That was around Christmas of 1963. But eventually Fritz made Esalen his home, and we even helped him build a house on the property.

My initial reaction to Fritz was not very good. As it turned out, Fritz had just experienced a heart attack before he came to Esalen, and apparently he thought he was going to die at any moment. Whether or not that was the reason, socially, he wasn't the most pleasant person to interact with, even when relatively healthy. So it took a couple of years – actually two years from the date of that first program – for me to start working with him. I started working with Fritz regularly in early 1966. I was in difficult space at that time because I had just ended a long-term relationship with a woman here at Esalen and I was feeling a lot of pain from that. So I dropped in on one of Fritz's groups. The first time we worked together was probably between Christmas of 1965 and New Year's of 1966. I immediately became very impressed by what Fritz was doing, and how different he was in a Gestalt group than my experience of him before, in regular conversation.

What impressed me about his work in groups was that he was insightful. He was present. He was compassionate – all the things I didn't consider him as being when I would see him in the Esalen Lodge or around the property. I was very impressed that this man, a psychiatrist, was doing such good work compared to what I had experienced, and compared to what happens today with most people who call themselves psychiatrists. As it turned out, Fritz was not qualified by the state of California to practice psychiatry. But, like all programs at Esalen, there is nothing done that is called "psychiatry." A person could be a psychiatrist, but they are not supposed to do psychiatry when they work at Esalen – they do experiential education, instead. So what Fritz did at Esalen essentially defined a new category of practice. But it really isn't accurate to say that this practice is new, because, even according to Fritz, Gestalt is as old as the world. It is a type of healing that is closer to so-called primitive societies, a process similar to a category of Shamanic healing and ritual. These approaches are more humane. They come into contact with people as real people, not as objects that need to be "fixed" in some way.

In any event, I started working with Fritz in early 1966. Then several years into that work I had my second mental break, which was largely the effect of not being able to finish the first one that I experienced thirteen years previously. So in the spring of 1969 I had another experience of a similar kind, most of which I was able to work through in Big Sur, but not at Esalen. I was actually staying with friends who had their own property, and who would protect the space for me to experience just what I was experiencing. After I got finished with that, which was in the summer of 1969, Fritz was already preparing to re-locate himself. He left Esalen after six years, and re-established himself at the Gestalt Institute of Canada at Adelaide College on Vancouver Island. I went up there and spent two of his last three teaching months with him. At the end of 1969 I left Canada and came back here to Esalen. Later, Fritz left Canada and went on a tour of Europe for the winter. He got sick in Europe, and then sicker still when he got back to the U.S. He never made it to Canada. He died in Chicago in March of 1970. In the months I spent with him in Canada there was a training institute that had been established for him. I went up there less to train with Fritz than to fully integrate my experience of the previous year. And that's when Fritz said to me, *"Dick it's time for you to go out and teach, and do your own groups."* So I started teaching Gestalt Practice when I got back to Esalen in 1970.

Gestalt, as I practice it, is similar in some respects to what I learned from Fritz, except that I made changes. Fritz made a strong point of not wanting disciples. As he put it, *"I do not want to train a lot of little Fritzes."* So what I got from Fritz, I put into my own wine bottle, so to speak. There are basic similarities in what I do, and there are a lot of differences, too. I'm Dick. I'm not Fritz. I have a lot of appreciation for Fritz. But Fritz's actual instruction was to, *"Take what I have and do your own thing with it."* He was very good that way, rather than having a standardized school. I don't think a standardized school of Gestalt really exists. There have been attempts at Gestalt Institutes. But I don't think Gestalt is something to be standardized, and I don't really care all that much about the Gestalt Institutes. I have never been particularly interested in them. I had my relationship with a master, and as far as I can see there was no reason for me to go to a Gestalt school, even if such a thing were possible. I don't think it is possible, in the sense of standardizing a product, to teach a particular idea about what Gestalt is or how to do it.

Just so we're all on the same page, let me back up and say that Gestalt is a German word that means *configuration*. Of course, nothing is ever perfectly defined. I asked a German fellow in one of my groups what the word meant, and he defined it as *figure*. It's like saying that there's a bridge over there, and you see the shadow of a man passing over it, but you don't see him clearly. When you see the figure, you are seeing a Gestalt. It's an impression of the whole. But it doesn't necessarily have to have a lot of clarity or detail. You don't have to see the man's eyes, or the way he buttons his shirt. You just see the figure – the configuration – in the sense of the verb *to configure*.

Fritz and Laura Perls came from Berlin. At the time, Laura, especially, was in contact with the various Gestalt psychologists who eventually left Germany before the war – most of them Jews. Many of them, like Kofka, Kohler, and Wertheimer, ended up teaching at the New School for Social

Research in New York during the early 1930's. They were doing experimental work, mostly with perceptual wholes. For example, you might see a single image in different configurations. In one particular perceptual experience, you might see a configuration that would look to you like two faces kissing. In another instance, you might see the configuration as a vase. Gestalt psychologists were working, mostly experimentally, in relation to these intriguing problems of perception. However, in what became Gestalt therapy, and then Gestalt Practice, we are interested in Gestalts and wholes, but not just as perceptual figures. In Gestalt Practice, the whole would include a perceptual element, a feeling element, and a sensational element. The total Gestalt, rather than merely a perceptual figure, might include an emotional figure, as in, "Now I'm feeling sadness," or a sensual figure, like "Now I'm feeling a pain in my forehead." There is the ability of the perceiver to choose, and to come into relationship with a field of experience in a way that can lead to greater and greater satisfaction. ... One simple example is to say, "Oh, now I'm hungry." With this awareness there is the discovery of, "Now I have the ability to choose." I can open the refrigerator and eat something, and then I'm no longer hungry. So we are always looking at this ability to form Gestalts, and then at letting go of Gestalts, in relationship to organic self-regulation. Fritz didn't use that expression very much, but Reich did. It is important to realize that Reich's socio-political interest was greater than Fritz's. And that perspective is also important to Gestalt Practice. So that's essentially what Gestalt is about – regulation both in an individual sense, and in a larger sense of social fields.

In order for me to describe how I do Gestalt Practice, I actually have to talk about what I don't do, because Gestalt is not a "doing." What Fritz called therapist and patient, that dyad, I refer to as reflector and initiator. The initiator is really the person who formerly was in the "patient" role. My function is simply to be available in a particular way to reflect and clarify whatever comes up in that person's process. I never define how a person should be. I'm available in a particular way, like a mirror – which is a good analogy. So the person remains responsible for his or her own experience. This is totally unlike the standard psychiatric approach – where you are put, if not in a jail cell, then certainly in a diagnostic pigeon hole of symptoms.

The central form that my work takes is the "open seat" group. In order to describe what happens, let's say that there is a group of fifteen people sitting in a circle. There are some basic awareness exercises that I give to the group. This is what I call "basic practice," which is attention to the body, to breath, to movement, to kinesthetic sensations, to sensations in the body – feeling states, emotion, thought, and images. And what's important is a mode of present centered contact that is brought to the experience, without judgment. So what's important and basic in the practice isn't about change. I'm not here to change anyone. What's important is contact. I function as an auxiliary to encourage and facilitate contact – namely, contact with one's own experience, not defined by anyone else from outside.

After the "basic practice" exercises, the opportunity is there for individuals to join me separately on the "open seat" – or not. The choice remains open. The authority to make the choice remains with what we call the initiator. It's quite different from psychiatry. The word "initiator" designates an active role, while the word "patient" is someone who, at least to me, is acted upon – and the therapist is the one who acts. Process is different. Process is active. So my Gestalt isn't "therapy." This is a "practice." This isn't something that a therapist does to a patient. It's what two people, in complementary roles, do together.

If someone moves up, onto the open seat next to me, what happens next is just whatever happens. I respond to whatever comes up – in a way to reflect and clarify. So the person might start out in some particular way. For example, often people start talking about a certain situation in their life.

In this practice there's a style of work, and there's a style of language. The style of work is different from talking about the past, or speculating about the future. It is designed to make everything real and present. So there may be a situation in your childhood – say you're thirteen years old and you're talking to your grandfather. Rather than telling me about it, you bring that into the present in imagination, and talk about that as if it were happening right now. So a continual instruction is simply to make experience real and present. That can also be true for a future situation, a future imagining. Imagine you are in San Francisco or in New Orleans. Where are you? What are you doing? Can you imagine being in a stadium watching an event, or in an auditorium listening to music? What is your experience? What is your experience of other people around you? My function as a reflector is to facilitate the initiator's imagination in a way that is present, rather than speculative in past or future tense. So a big part of Gestalt language is using the present tense. This is also true in dream work. Rather than talking about a dream or attempting to analyze, you enter the dream imagery, and become the various parts – no matter how unworldly. You can become an animal – you can become a house – but everything is present centered, and handled by entering and experiencing, rather than talking about it from a distance.

The purpose of the practice is not to force change. However, most people who participate in the process do seem to accomplish something, because they want to change somehow, in order to resolve something. There's something for them to get out of the way. But this practice is really a practice of contacting what is, and letting change be something that happens on its own, rather than something that is made to happen, or even has to happen. A person might come up with a certain idea of how they want to change. They enter their experience, and the change that happens – that they actually find satisfying – is quite different from what they would have imagined. So to be open to what is, rather than having to define what has to be, is very important to this practice. It's important for the person to have that attitude, and also for the person who is in the reflective relationship to have that attitude.

Let's say you come up to work with me. I'm not defining how you have to be, although I might have some ideas as I see you work. But again, the authority remains with the initiator. I'm not going to push you in a direction, even if I might say to myself, *"I know this is what's going to be 'good' for you."* If I said that out loud, then the authority would come back to me. But my only authority is in being able to define the structure of Gestalt Practice, itself. You remain the authority for your own experience; you remain the authority for the choices that you make.

Part of my intention is to reflect in such a way as to assist people to intensify or deepen their awareness. My function is to be present for people almost like a mirror. In other words, there is much you can do yourself, so I am present for you as a mirror.

Here's an illustration I can give of the relationship. – If a guy wants to shave, he can actually do it without a mirror. Yet, having a mirror is going to help him in the process of shaving. It's not that he couldn't do it by himself. But the mirror helps. That's a pretty good analogy of what I do as the reflector.

One of my primary functions is what I call "helping you to hold the avoided figure." You might find yourself getting angry, for example, or resentful, or sad – things you might define as something that you shouldn't be. I would just say, *"Hey, hold on a minute. Contact that sense of anger or sadness or irritation, or whatever it is."* And I leave it to your own experience. You can choose not to follow my direction. But if you do, what you find, most times, is that with contact comes a certain type of self-regulation. In other words, if you feel sad you can allow crying, and by allowing crying you may no longer feel sad. That is a change that is allowed to happen. So what's primary here is not the goal of, "Don't be sad." It's simply, "Contact your sadness." Of course, you may stay sad – there are no guarantees.

For me, there are three main elements of Gestalt. I call them The Three Jewels of Gestalt Practice. They are: Awareness, Choice and Trust. The trust element is found in your power of self-regulation, given the exercise of your ability to contact experience, and you ability to choose. The more you discover that trust, the less you need another person, even like me – and much less so, certainly, will you need the average therapist.

What is primary is not any specific goal of striving to achieve a particular state. There are few people who come into a group without wanting some change or some resolution. So that's always going to be there. I'm not trying to make something bad out of that. But the practice, as a practice, is one of contact, and not change. This takes a certain reorientation. So in a session someone might want to resolve something. There's some other way that they want it to be. But what you might notice is that the more they want to change, the more they try to keep things in the 'why' framework, rather than the 'how' framework – the more they tie themselves up and effectively remain the same. So it's almost a paradox; it's almost like Aikido. There's a certain kind of Taoist principle operating, so that simply by allowing, change happens naturally. With allowing and with contact, rather than by forcing, change happens. There really is a positive philosophy of non-forcing or non-doing involved here, and an openness to what happens – rather than having a firm definition of how you should be, even if that's something like, "I shouldn't be sad," or "I shouldn't be angry."

One of the goals or values of the Gestalt attitude is moving from environmental support to self-support. It is implicit in the values of the self-help movement – values like clarity, simplicity and honesty. You can think of these in terms of individual self-support. And you can also think of them in terms of group self-support, where there isn't an outside dependence, outside of something that is an organic whole. You're not seeking "expert advice." A good example is what might be done in a cooperative housing community. You might ask for residents to contribute five or ten hours of work a week, so that people can effectively support themselves. By doing it that way, you are able to strengthen the household and charge much less than you would have to otherwise. Normally, you might have to call a plumber. But you're better off if someone in the cooperative house knows about plumbing, and then you don't have to bother with an outside plumber who charges so much. It's the same as not having a shift of cooks and waiters to serve you a meal. You can do it yourself. However, self-support doesn't deny a certain degree of functional environmental support. As Fritz would put it, "You learn to wipe your own ass," either as an individual, or as a creative, self-supportive group of people.

So self-support is a value in Gestalt. Awareness is also a value. Awareness is a good thing in itself. Fully living life is a value. There is inherent vitality in living life. Fritz was a patient of Wilhelm Reich for ten months. So some of the Reichian values, like vitality and aliveness, are implicit in Gestalt values. The values in the larger culture are what Reich referred to as the

Emotional Plague, in the sense that the implicit norm in the social system is, "Life can't be trusted." Gestalt practice says, "Trust in Life! Trust in Self Support!" Trust in life, awareness, initiative and choice! What about honesty? Certainly there is self-honesty. The values of encounter are openness and honesty. The values in Gestalt are openness and honesty both in service of the organism, and in being able to choose. But there are times when being honest isn't functional.

Generally, you have to be able to trust. So trust is a primary value. Awareness, choice and trust are all Gestalt values. With trust comes openness and honesty – trust in yourself and learning to trust the other. I have to be able to trust myself enough, and you enough, to know that when I'm working you're not going to turn me in for some offense, or call a psychiatrist or a cop on me. On the other hand, I may have some good reason not to be open and honest with some people. And again, it comes back to choice, but in the interest of life and vitality. And as relationships become more and more established, we do learn to trust.

So I came to call the version of Gestalt I teach, "Gestalt Practice." In my practice I tried to combine everything I had been exploring, experiencing, and experimenting with over the years. Everything that provided ground for people to explore altered states in different ways – and also for me to explore those states. This approach is a combination of Gestalt and body work, and in some cases the use of psychotropic substances. Everything about these things, singly and collectively, have contributed to the formation of how I sit here, both theoretically, practically, and from the point of view of who I am able to be.

The main thing about it is the way I sit here. That's it. That is the way I hold space, and what it means to have somebody hold space in this way – someone who sits in trust and is basically fearless about what is going to emerge.

Two important aspects of my world that were intimately involved in the development of my practice are: first, that Gestalt Practice serves as a vehicle for practicing the principle: *maximum availability, minimum coercion.* And second, in creating Gestalt Practice, I was attempting to provide for others what would have been most useful for me during my own psychological difficulties. Both these aspects serve self-reparative psychological functions. So what I am saying this morning, rather than being an attempt at being an exhaustive, comprehensive review, is designed to give you the flavor of my approach as an extension of my personal phenomenology.

As I acknowledged before, there are basic similarities and basic differences between Gestalt Practice and Fritz Perls' Gestalt therapy. The basic similarities included: first, adopting the principle of organismic self-regulation and the realization of personal autonomy that principle embodies; second, a commitment to awareness in the here and now as a healing means and end; and third, the adoption of many of the basic Gestalt techniques.

So first, I embraced and adopted the concept of organismic self-regulation. Like Fritz, I relied upon the autonomous "wisdom of the organism" inherent in the concept of "organismic self-regulation" that emerges when someone is in full contact with their experience.

And then there's the idea that I'm leaving this to your own experience. You can choose not to follow my direction, but if you do – if you slow down and enter – what you find most of the time is that with contact comes a certain type of self-regulation.

The second similarity is, like my mentor, I am committed to awareness in the here and now as a means and end. The root of Gestalt therapy is Fritz's: *how* and *now*. When I explain the origins of Gestalt Practice, I often refer to the following statement by Fritz. He said something like: *"There are two legs upon which Gestalt therapy walks: now and how."* The essence of the theory of Gestalt is in the understanding of these two words. *Now* covers all that exists. The past is no more, the future is not yet. Now includes the balance of being here – experiencing, involvement, phenomenon, awareness. *How* covers everything that is structure – behavior – all that is actually going on – the ongoing *process*. All the rest is irrelevant – computing, apprehending, and so on.

In Gestalt Practice as in Gestalt therapy, "*how, now*" is supported through the use of the continuum of awareness: the actual "reporting of your experience, in this moment." As I point out in groups, the basic reporting of experience can be broken down into two questions. The first has to do with *being*: "What is your experience now?' The second has to do with *doing*: "What are you doing now?" What are you doing in relation to the experience you are having? The question, "What is your experience now?" could be further supported by facilitating the ability to fully contact, to be able to enter, to then allow, to fully accept, and finally to be able to express that experience. The question, "What are you doing now?" can be broken down into one further question, "How do you do this?" I maintain that after full and clear contact with one's experience, and what one does in relation to that experience, other possibilities will emerge.

The third similarity is that Gestalt Practice employs many of Fritz's basic techniques. Those techniques include the "empty chair," the continuum of awareness, and the use of "Gestalt language" – namely: making "I" statements, talking directly *to* rather than *about*, not asking *why* but *how*, describing rather than explaining, and talking in concrete and specific terms rather than in general or abstract terms – all of these are designed to bring the person working into more direct, experiential contact with themselves in the here and now.

Fritz's five basic Gestalt questions also served as a cornerstone of Gestalt Practice. Namely: 1."What are you experiencing?" 2."What do you want to do?' 3."What do you want from me?" 4. "What are you avoiding?" and 5."What are you actually doing?" To these basic five questions, I add a sixth of my own, 6." How should I know?" Actually, as I often repeat: "I really only say three things: What is your experience now? What are you doing now? *and*, How should I know?"

There are also basic differences between Fritz's Gestalt therapy and my Gestalt Practice. As I said earlier, I often use the analogy of putting what I learned from Fritz into my own bottle. Rather than imitating Fritz, I felt I had Fritz's blessing to make Gestalt my own.

The main features that separate Gestalt Practice from Gestalt therapy include the following: first, an emphasis on doing Gestalt as a form of *practice*; second, a greater emphasis on the body; third, a blending of concepts from Buddhist meditation practice with Gestalt; and fourth, a specific emphasis on the organization of experience through a paradigm that I called: *message-program-filter* or MPF for short.

Gestalt in my model is a shared lifestyle, rather than something that one occasionally does by appointment in the office of a professional therapist. So the first difference from

Gestalt therapy is the ongoing communitarian nature of Gestalt Practice, no doubt facilitated by the residential nature of life here at Esalen Institute.

The second feature that helps to differentiate Gestalt Practice is my greater emphasis on the body. My practice differs from Fritz's approach by adding a lot of work about body and breath. Fritz was brilliant with extremities and my work is more toward the core. I really did think that Fritz was brilliant about bringing awareness to hands and arms, legs, eyes, ears – while I focus more on the physical core. I want to be very clear about that difference between us. And I think there are some huge differences just because of who we are as people. Fritz had three heart attacks – physically and in a lot of other ways, he was husbanding his energy. The fact is, both physically and energetically, I'm very athletic, still a highly charged guy and my work focuses on that physicality a whole lot more.

I'm a body-based person and use my own physicality as a grounding tool in helping to manage my own subjective experience. I often use this physicality in doing Gestalt work. I might hold, restrain, or use my body as something a person could push against, or test their strength against, if that served a meaningful purpose. I'm fairly fearless in this regard, though I'm always very, very respectful and protective of the other person.

I also put direct focus on the body core by focusing direct attention on the breath with a process I call "basic practice" which I mentioned earlier. I define basic practice as "becoming established in body and breath" which I suggest as a way to begin every session, and a place to return to, if needed, for grounding throughout the session. I usually begin my Gestalt groups by asking group members to participate in a short guided meditation, which I usually introduced with a variation of the following instruction: *"Can you be aware of? ... without having to change in any way ... the inflow and outflow of your breath ... the movement of your body with breath ... and any sensation state in relation to breath."* Basic Practice is attention to breath, to movement, to kinesthetic sensations, to sensations in the body – feeling state, emotion, thought, image. And what's important is a mode of present-centered contact, which doesn't judge what is brought to that.

I usually work with people individually in a group setting, with a more relaxed context that I call the "open seat," in order to distinguish my practice from Fritz's highly charged "hot seat" environment. After becoming established in body and breath through "basic practice" I usually start individual sessions with continuum of awareness, by having the person who is working, report: *"Now I am aware of... and now I am aware of... etc."*

The third feature that distinguished Gestalt Practice is my blend of Buddhist practice with Gestalt. My Gestalt work is also part of an ongoing personal spiritual practice. Although Fritz occasionally referred to Zen in his work and writings and had some passing knowledge of Buddhism, Gestalt Practice is more spiritual, because one of my committed practices is Buddhism. From my Buddhist practice comes one important technique and one important concept that helped to differentiate Gestalt Practice from Gestalt therapy. First, from Buddhist meditation practice I adopted the technique of focusing direct attention on the breath, as I already described. Second, following the Buddhist precept of the "wisdom of equality" I adopted the concept that, *It makes no difference what the figure being worked on is – the quality of awareness you bring to the figure makes a big difference."*

For me, an extremely important concept in Gestalt Practice is bringing the highest possible quality of awareness to whatever emerges as figure. "If you do this" *(I often say when I'm teaching Gestalt)* "then you can't do it wrong" because you can always take one step back and bring awareness to whatever's happening. If you are resisting any figure, then you can always take a step back and focus on the resistance, as figure.

Unlike Fritz's theatrical style, my Gestalt work is much more meditative, focusing primarily on the quality of awareness brought to moment-to-moment experience. As I'm fond of saying: *"Coming out with something is secondary to making the contact with whatever is, with clarity, and making it real and present."*

When asked to describe the difference between my approach and Fritz's, I acknowledge a deeper kind of availability. Like I say, Fritz had a background in theater and acting. I don't, and I don't have a whole lot of interest in theater, really. Fritz wouldn't stay with a person as long in process as I would, so there was less permission. Permission is either given explicitly or implied. There was less implied permission to go deeply into an emotion. So I'm more available than Fritz at what I would call a deeper level. *And I'm probably not as entertaining!"*

The fourth distinguishing characteristic of Gestalt Practice is my deep and abiding respect for the subjective reality of the person I'm working with. Unlike Fritz, who was known to be quite dismissive or sometimes even brutal in his so-called "circus" demonstration sessions, I am very concerned about the psychological safety of the people I work with, in keeping with my precept: *"maximum availability, minimum coercion."* One of my favorite instructions that I use to help teach Gestalt Practice, is the following: *"As the reflector, create a safe place for the initiator so they can face unsafe places."* At other times I will say: *"Your job as reflector is to create the space – not fill it – create the space so the initiator can fill it."* For me there are three essentials: no judgment, no coercion, and no analysis.

Combining what I inherited from Fritz with my own personal "twist" to Gestalt – namely: attention to breath and emphasis on the quality of awareness, I created a simple structure from which I operate in doing Gestalt Practice. Operating within that structure enables me and others to successfully work with the staff here at Esalen – people with whom I had multiple relationships every day. My ground rules for Gestalt Practice are like a sport which can be played with a predictable rule structure, but also with a great amount of freedom. If I ever step outside of the Gestalt Practice structure, which is extremely rare, I say something like the following: *"I'm now leaving my role as reflector and speaking to you as Dick Price."*

It also helps me to make one further distinction between Gestalt Practice and Gestalt therapy. I distinguish between what I call "Acid Gestaltists" and "Soft Gestaltists." There are what I call, conceptually, two categories of Gestaltists. One does Acid Gestalt. They tell you how you should be and they frustrate. Fritz would talk about skillful frustration. Not everyone doing the work frustrates skillfully. If I frustrate you skillfully, then you are almost forced to find another way beyond your usual neurotic defenses. This works well for some people, both as initiators and reflectors – or what "professionals" call patient and therapist. Acid Gestaltists tend to be confrontational and sarcastic. And then there's what I call Soft Gestaltists, the Aikido Gestaltists. They're simply present with whatever happens without having to put in their own judgments or frustrate. My own attitude is that you frustrate yourself enough. I don't have to frustrate you. All I need to do is be present and reflect your self-frustrations back, and let you choose whether you want to continue to do that or want to find another way. I don't have to be your judge. Again, there are strong echoes of my precept, *maximum availability, minimum coercion*, in this soft Gestalt approach.

The fifth distinctive aspect of Gestalt Practice is the message-program filter, or MPF paradigm I formulated as a way of looking at how experience is meaningfully organized. The MPF paradigm reflects upon enduring organizations of experience, or what contemporary Gestaltists have referred to as ongoing structures of ground – the organization of the background, in figure/ground terms, out of which figures conditionally arise.

So I developed a simple paradigm for conceptualizing important features of the way that people I work with organize their experience. And I called this paradigm "message-program-filter." I always keep this paradigm in the back of my mind when I work with people. In many ways, I believe this MPF paradigm provides answers to contemporary criticisms of the Perlsian Gestalt model. In that respect my MPF paradigm is a radical departure from the Gestalt therapy I inherited from Fritz. I acknowledge that in the following this model I break one of my own maxims. I say that, *"For me there are three essentials: no judgment, no coercion, and no analysis."* But I break my own rule when I lay out my paradigm of message-program-filter.

I haven't published or written about this paradigm. And to the best of my understanding there isn't any reference to it published in the Gestalt literature. That's fine. My MPF is based upon my own understanding of process, and put into very simple language – real simple because I want it to stay simple. It's important for the concept to be properly assimilated, because it serves as a bridge between Gestalt and other kinds of work. At the same time I like to say, *"It's nothing new."* How could it be? After all, I formulated it after years of doing and observing Gestalt sessions here at Esalen. So it's not like something I either give credit or take credit for. It's just natural.

The MPF paradigm is a shorthand method of formulating developmental influences on the organization of experience. According to the structure of the paradigm, messages communicated to a child by primary caregivers are assimilated and transformed into powerful programs of action. Over time, such programs of action generalize to situations that extend far beyond their original context, becoming filters through which the world is viewed. Though very useful in their original context, these recurrent patterns of perception and action cause the world to be seen, and acted upon, as if the original conditions remained as current conditions of the interpersonal field. The object of Gestalt Practice is to bring reflective awareness to bear upon the repetitive patterns of perception and action that the MPF represent – so that creative alternatives can emerge, be supported, and become viable. That's the general idea. So now let me walk you through a more detailed account of my MPF paradigm:

First there's the message. In the MPF framework, the term message is used to conceptualize the powerful early messages communicated by primary caregivers about life, the world, how a person is, and how they need to be. Specifically, how one should think, behave and act. The top three sources of messages are: mother, father, and the relationship between them. Messages are conveyed both consciously and unconsciously. In fact, conscious messages can be at odds with unconscious ones. It's like what parents say, compared to what they actually do, and unconscious messages are often the more powerful of the two. Common bearers of such messages – other than primary caretakers – are relatives, friends, the culture and powerful events. That's the message.

In the MPF paradigm, program is used to conceptualize how early messages are put into action. Program includes both how the messages are construed – consciously and unconsciously – and the action plan that is developed in relation to them. The strength of these "programs of action" is directly related to what I refer to as "the three S-s: safety, security, and survival." That's the program.

Filter, in the MPF framework, refers to how the program is actualized over time. Programs of action tend to generalize to situations that are far beyond the original context, eventually becoming a filter through which the world is seen. The programs of action that children develop in their families of origin are very useful. They usually represent the best, or maybe even the *only* choice the child could have made to ensure his or her safety, security, and survival. Though useful in their original context, such programs of action can be inappropriate to, or even at direct odds with, current needs or the current situation in which those needs could potentially be met. Filters can keep the individual from growing and maturing by causing the world to be seen, and acted in, as if the original family of origin and its conditions and limitations are still in effect. As I often put the problem: *"It's behaving now as if it were back then."*

Message, program, and filter combine to form strong, recurrent patterns of perception and action. The strength of these recurring patterns is directly related to the extent to which the initially patterns created a felt sense of safety, security, and survival. The objective of awareness practice is to become aware of our various patterns of perceiving and acting – the filters through which we see the world. This awareness is facilitated by recognizing how the original program of action once served us, in the sense of its being the best thing the child could have done in the given circumstances. I called this: *"appreciating the power of the program."* When the power of the program is seen clearly – including seeing how the pattern may not serve us in the current and different situations – alternatives can emerge. As I say to practitioners, *"all three – message, program, and filter together – become a pattern, and hopefully we can come to a fourth: the creative alternative."*

An example I use to illustrate this MPF paradigm is that of a very young girl who, to please her father and get his approval and attention, is encouraged to perform for him in some way. The message, never actually stated by the father, is that: "if you perform for me in ways I approve, you will get my support, love, and attention." The program of action the girl develops to please her father then becomes a ritualized performance that they share. The need to give a performance of some kind in order to get approval begins to generalize to other situations, and gradually becomes a filter through which the world is seen. What was once encouraged becomes something that the girl unconsciously thinks is required of her in order to get approval, to be liked, to be loved, or to get what she wants or needs from others. She does not think about it consciously, because the performance becomes an unconscious, habitual response pattern. The message, program and filter become an entrenched pattern, which the girl brings, in varying degrees, to every interpersonal situation.

In the MPF model, this particular pattern, played out over time, would lead to a split between "being" and "doing." In other words, I get what I need – attention, approval, love, safety, security, or survival – by doing – performing in some way and not for simply being who I am. In practice, the "creative alternative" of feeling validated for being, rather than doing, needs to be supported. Through that support, both being and doing can become valid and eventually more or less equal possibilities. In practice, I emphasize the need to see the pattern clearly – *this is what I do and how it actually was useful* – as a prelude to the formation of a "creative alternative." As I often say, *"You have to go all the way into the pattern for new possibilities to exist."*

We all have many MPF patterns that we habitually use – many filters through which we see the world. The work of practice is to bring these patterns into conscious awareness so that creative alternatives can emerge, be supported, and become viable.

So there are two critical, interrelated gaps in obsolescent forms of Gestalt therapy, which are resolved by the Gestalt Practice model. First, the old form of Gestalt therapy lacked a coherent developmental theory. Second, Perls' Gestalt therapy tended to ignore and devalue the importance of human relationships in both developmental and practice realms. The MPF paradigm addresses, at least partially, both these gaps and serves as a bridge between old Gestalt therapy and the new Gestalt Practice. One method for redressing gaps in the old form of Gestalt therapy is accomplished by re-emphasizing Martin Buber's contributions to Gestalt, and another is by incorporating ideas about developmental phenomena from contemporary forms of relationship analysis, like object relations, into Gestalt Practice.

Martin Buber's I-Thou relationship has been recognized by contemporary theorists as forming the basis for effective interpersonal encounters. By highlighting Buber's I-Thou relationship in the context of dialogic relations between reflector and initiator, contemporary Gestalt practitioners have attempted to establish the relationship, itself, as the central factor in Gestalt Practice. Healing occurs through meeting in genuine dialogue. According to Buber, the chief characteristic of genuine dialogue *"is that each should regard their partner as the very one they are."* I become aware of you, aware that you are different, essentially different from myself, in the unique way which is peculiar to you, and I accept who I see, so that I can fully direct what I say to you as the person you are.

Dialogue, according to Buber, is at the center of psychological and spiritual development because, as he said: *"All real living is meeting."* An I-Thou process, requiring an I-Thou attitude, has largely been ignored by Gestalt therapists, while the I-Thou moment – a "peak moment" of full being-to-being contact – is central in Gestalt Practice. This is because dialogue is part of the invisible ground of practice, essential and always there, yet most often unnoticed. Buber's philosophy of dialogue serves as a logical corrective to the Perlsian model's individualistic bent and its overemphasis on personal awareness as the primary curative factor. The MPF paradigm facilitates an I-Thou attitude by encouraging the "reflector" to view the "initiator" from a perspective that is inclusive of their subjective world – by imagining the "filter" through which they view the world, and its developmental origins. In addition, I try to maintain a deep and abiding respect for the validity of the subjective reality of the other person. That is what underpins the formation of an I-Thou attitude as the ground out of which genuine dialogue can take place. Buber's I-Thou attitude presupposes an acceptance of the other, in their full "otherness," which is the fundamental attitude I take toward those I work with.

The MPF Gestalt Practice paradigm expands the parameters of the Perlsian Gestalt therapy model, providing some answers to contemporary criticisms of Gestalt therapy. In order to utilize MPF, the Gestalt practitioner has to think very differently than the Perlsian approach. First, MPF makes the practitioner consider the structure of the ground, and not just the emerging figure. When the practitioner has to account for how the ground is structured, then relational and developmental factors naturally emerge as prominent features. Second, MPF facilitates viewing the experience of the initiator from a perspective within, rather than outside, their own subjective world, by having to imagine the filter through which that world is seen and how that filter was created. Third, MPF provides a perspective for looking at practice over a much longer time frame than the Gestalt therapy model would suggest, or Perls would acknowledge. Fourth, MPF moves the focus of practice from emotional expression towards an exploration of the meaning of past and present emotional experience. Fifth, MPF provides a frame for identifying principles around which experience is organized – it's a way of mapping the subjective world. Sixth, and finally, by encouraging the investigation of early relational interaction patterns the MPF paradigm also encourages an object relations view of development, thereby suggesting use of that perspective for Gestalt Practice.

Actually, I inherited an *intrapersonal* view of process from my mentor, Fritz Perls. It's a view I have often described as exclusively focusing on the "intrapersonal" or internal dimensions of experience. Trust in relationships, considering my own personal history, was something that did not come easy for me. However, my MPF framework suggests other possibilities. If relationships are the primary causal factors in creating organizations of experience in MPF terms, then by implication relationships can serve as reorganizing factors as well.

You have to be able to trust. Trust is a primary value. I would say awareness, choice, and trust are all primary values. With trust comes openness and honesty. Trust in yourself, and learn to trust the other. In the past, in my own life, I may have had some good reasons not to be open and honest with some people. Again it comes back to choice – in the interest of life and vitality. As my relationships became more and more established here at Esalen, I learned to trust. Ideally, eventually, we do learn to trust.

The development of the message-program-filter, or MPF paradigm provides a way of conceptualizing how experience is subjectively organized, which logically leads to possibilities that are beyond the vulnerabilities and defenses of both myself and my mentor Fritz Perls. Recognizing the limitations inherent in the realization of personal autonomy and self-versus-environment support, we arrive at that inescapable conclusion, if the full implications of MPF are followed to their logical ends. Put simply, the MPF paradigm leads toward a developmental and relational view of practice. In so doing, the MPF paradigm can be regarded as a bridge between obsolescent Gestalt therapy and more contemporary forms of practice which emphasize developmental and relational aspects of experience, like for instance object relations theory.

A final bridge between old Gestalt therapy and my Gestalt Practice involves ideas held by "professionals" about what is "treatable." I do not consider any diagnostic category that is "untreatable." In fact, I don't believe in the usefulness of diagnostic categorization at all. It's a gimmick for distancing yourself from real people. Something I do consider useful is an absolute respect for the validity of the subjective experience of the other person – a respect that holds that no subjective organization of experience is any more true or more valid than any other. In my practice I remain wide open in this regard – anything could be real – anything can be talked about that is capable of being experienced. I have absolutely no investment in having experience conform to any psychological system or to common-sense notions of reality. If someone I work with is experiencing something that is truly novel, something that does not fit any psychological system I know about, so much the better! It is precisely this kind of attitude that extends the limits of what was considered to be "treatable," as well as my own personal values.

I consider the full range of human experience, including the so-called "psychoses," to be worthwhile subjects of practice, if a reflector strives to comprehend the subjective truth in the initiators arguably delusional ideas, and communicates this understanding in a form the initiator can use. If a reflector can do this successfully, experiences of self-loss, fragmentation and disintegration that have come to express specific forms of invalidation, accommodation and usurpation, can be made intelligible, facilitating a possible restoration and consolidation of a fragmenting subjective world. From this perspective it is the attempt to comprehend the person from within their own subjective world that extends the limits of what has been considered relatable by commercial psychotherapy.

I worked with many, many people who therapists would have labeled psychotic. I did Gestalt Practice sessions with them, hiked with them, and protected them while they were going through their states. In my basic stance, there is always a fundamental regard and respect for the other person and the belief that there is a reaching out for some kind of needed contact beneath the surface craziness. The kind of acceptance and support I offer to those who are suffering a so-called "psychosis" is the exactly what I found missing in my own experience. – Treat initiators with respect. Don't care about the other things that people are judged by. Trust in process.

I can say that now I am never really disappointed with any Gestalt session. At one time, this might not have been true, because I can see how much might happen when someone willingly contacts or enters the process of Gestalt play. This contactful type of session is likely to be a lot more satisfying. A person who really contacts their experience feeds back with a degree of clarity. This person then is someone who willingly plays the Gestalt game – for example, by entering into a dream image, instead of saying, *"This is ridiculous; how can I become a cow? I'm not really a cow,"* or, *"I'm not my mother."* So someone who enters the Gestalt form with a sense of vitality and play is going to be a lot more satisfying to me, especially when I can see a person entering into, say, sadness – going into grief work, and coming out the other side with a degree of clarity and openness and sense of aliveness. That's satisfying for the person, and it's satisfying for me. On the other hand, learning not to be disappointed is a kind of equanimity that I have learned over the years.

As I say this, I realize it has been almost sixteen years, now, that I have been doing Gestalt work as a reflector. Of course, I still do it both as an initiator and a reflector. I've been doing it as a reflector since 1970, and as an initiator since 1966. That's nineteen years altogether. Nineteen years as what I call an initiator, and sixteen years as what I call a reflector. What I have learned to do during this period of time is to make reflecting into an awareness practice. So part of my ideal as reflector is to make Gestalt a practice of awareness for myself while I'm reflecting. Actually, that's true for both parts of the dyad. Both partners, it must be remembered, are doing the practice together, rather than one person doing something to the other. And in the practice there is an equality – the Buddhists call it the wisdom of equality – in the sense that equal attention is given to whatever emerges. So it doesn't really matter whether the work is what ordinarily would be a really interesting and vital session, compared to one that is not so interesting and not so vital. I can bring the same clarity of consciousness to either one. Whatever has been presented to me is an object of my awareness, just like a pain in my arm or a really good feeling in my heart. One is not so pleasant. One is very pleasant. I can bring attention equally to either object. I do that with people, too. Every session for me is equally an opportunity for my own practice. And in this way, I am no longer left disappointed by a session. Whoever shows up is providing me with an opportunity for practice. I can be equally grateful for the most "disappointing" session, and the most "alive" session.

Of course, to be honest about it, I'm not quite at the point, yet, where I find all session equally satisfying. But I'm working on it! There's less of a difference now. And I am able to maintain nourishment for myself by following the basic practice that I give to other people. That practice consists of being aware and centered in my own breath, taking responsibility for my own experience, and being available in a particular way that doesn't push and doesn't need to have anything happen from outside. And yes, there is pleasure and satisfaction in sessions where that 'certain something' does happen. But I wouldn't use the word 'disappointment' now, when it doesn't. There's relative satisfaction. Any session is satisfying. It's just that some sessions are more satisfying than others! It might be nice for all sessions to be equally satisfying, but I certainly don't expect that. And by not expecting that, I save myself from disappointment. All sessions are experiments. People find out what works for them. Gestalt is a style that is fine for some people, and not so fine for others.

So in comparison to Fritz, my approach is quite different, in part because Fritz's background in theater. He wouldn't stay with a person in process as long as I do. There was less permission with Fritz. Permission is given either explicitly or implicitly. There was less implied permission to go deeply into emotion with Fritz. So I'm more available at what I would call a deeper lever than Fritz.

My problems with Acid Gestalt are coercion and judgment. If someone had a pattern of behavior that was frustrating both to others and also to the person using it, Fritz would attempt to block that. But Fritz had the skill to be able to use frustration in a different way than a lot of other people. I've witnessed some Gestaltists who automatically use frustration as a style, rather than simply being present for experience.

Not everyone who does this work frustrates skillfully. This works well with some people, both as initiators and reflectors. So there are the Acid Gestaltists, who tend to be confrontational and sarcastic. Jim Simkin is a good example of that, I think. Soft Gestaltists are simply present with whatever happens, without having to add their own judgments, or frustrate. All I need to do is be present to reflect your self-frustrations back, and then let you have a choice of whether you want to continue to do that, or to find another way. And I don't have to be your judge.

One of Fritz's favorite films was Roshomon, which is the story of robbery and rape, told from four different perspectives – the alleged rapist, the woman, the husband, and a beggar who's looking on from the bushes. In the same way, there are different perspectives on how to do Gestalt. So there are people who, for me, are Gestaltist, but they might not even know it. They probably have no connection to Fritz. And Fritz, himself, was also a composite of Karen Horney, Charlotte Selver and Wilhelm Reich – yet he was very definitely Fritz. There's a kind of osmosis by which, somehow, all of these projects connect or don't connect. And so, for me, the most important single element is one's own personal approach, one's own style, whatever theoretical label is used.

What I'm teaching as Gestalt Practice probably doesn't look anything like the kind of Gestalt that other people are teaching. In many ways it doesn't look anything like what Fritz did, either. I sometimes imagine that if some of the people who consider themselves Fritz's students saw what I do, they would be appalled that I actually call it Gestalt. But if you think I'm not doing Gestalt, then neither was Fritz! The important thing is to be able to recognize the practice for what it is, and then enter it. Seen from that perspective, what I do looks very similar to what Fritz did. Actually, Fritz's problem was that it was very rare for him to have someone who fully entered into the practice. In fact, one of the first things that Fritz told me was that he felt lucky if he had one or two people in a group who were really interested in what he had to teach them. And that's one of the reasons he was so acid, because he felt that what he did was so obvious, yet people would not pick up on it, and so he felt that the main thing people were into doing was frustrating him. But when there are a few people who can almost taste what is there for them, then that is, in itself, rewarding enough.

It would probably be fair to say that my wife, Christine, and I – the two of us – have been the primary teachers of

Gestalt Practice here at Esalen for these many years since Fritz left. And although we have developed a Soft Gestalt approach, I would say that Fritz used it first. At least Fritz did when Fritz was in that mode. I chose to pick up on the soft approach from him, and evolved that – rather than the other form, which was also Fritz. So far as I know, nobody else developed the same kind of style that we have. Richard Olney and Cherie Coy do something they call Self-Acceptance Training. It sounds like it may be very similar, although I have never watched them work.

I don't actually use the phrase "Soft Gestalt" very often for this work. We call it Gestalt Practice, as an alternative to Gestalt therapy. That change happened, immediately, when I started doing Gestalt workshops in early 1970. At first we dropped the 'therapy' part, and we would just say Gestalt workshops. In fact, the word therapy is pretty much edited out of the Esalen catalog, although it occasionally sneaks back in. For me, therapy has the connotation that, if I'm a therapist then I'm someone who does something to you, from a position of superior authority, which is just the kind of mind-set we want to get rid of. Instead, what is happening when you work with me is that I'm present, and we're present together, in a mutual practice. In a way, we're doing this together. And the authority for your experience remains with you, whereas the authority for my experience remains with me.

Besides Fritz, my other major teacher, in the early days, was Alan Watts. Alan wasn't anyone you'd want to work with, personally. That was not what Alan did. But as I said earlier, just in terms of a particular type of mind-set, he was very important to me in the 1950s. Reich is another person who has been very influential for me. I actually met his daughter, Eva Reich, here at Esalen. And there is also Rajneesh, who was very influential for me, at least in his writings. For one thing, in Gestalt we talk about the issue of movement from "environmental support to self support." Fritz would almost overemphasize this, because he was so committed not to be dependent on anyone else, and his theory reflects, to some degree, his own personal pathology. One thing that I liked about Rajneesh was that he moved from dependence to independence, and then to the recognition of the need for interdependence. That's more the position I want to emphasize. Don't make a dichotomy out of environmental self-support. Instead, move to a "relative self-support" that creatively and correctly uses environmental support, which is necessary for one's own growth and development.

In contrast, some people seem to say that you are almost totally responsible for everything that happens to you. This is the EST-ian position. There is a certain awkwardness in this position. It's quite different, for me, to be responsible in the sense that Fritz used the term – "response-ability" – in other words, to be able to respond to one's situation. The other sense gets to be almost an absurd position. Will Schutz went off on this EST position. For example, if I was napalmed in Vietnam, presumable I was creating that – I was choosing that. To me this isn't the meaning of responsibility. It goes over to a kind of blame position. It misses the point. Schutz really went off on the position in which we are even responsible for creating a birth defect. In Gestalt, responsibility is a position of acceptance. And this is what it means for me now – a sense in which issues of blame don't really enter in the same way. I think that the EST sense has been picked up on a lot, and made a little absurd.

In Gestalt we talk about desired directions. And one of those directions is the movement from environmental support to self-support – with a recognition of interdependence. In other words, it is not a position of absolute self-support, in the sense that I don't need anyone else, but the recognition of need within certain boundaries. And part of self-support is knowledge of when, and when not, to use environmental support, so as not to make a rigid dichotomy between the two. The general direction of Gestalt is to move, more and more, from environmental support toward a position of self-support. So the more I allow you the opportunity to utilize your own capacities, the better off you are.

For this reason, the way I see it, there really aren't any pitfalls or dangers in the use of Gestalt Practice. I don't see any potential problems in the softer Gestalt approaches. Because, for me, Gestalt Practice, instead of being a therapy, is simply an alternative way for people to be present with one another, in a way that is likely to be quite a bit more nourishing than many of the ways that people tend to be together. The practice is to be available for another's experience, just as that experience is, without trying to define it to be a particular way. I think that you could look at Gestalt as simply a way to be present with yourself in the world, and a way to be present with another person or a group of people.

I encourage people to do Gestalt with one another, on their own. There are many people who have been to a Gestalt Practicum at Esalen. We don't call them "trainings." Instead, what happens is this – a more experienced person sits-in with a group of people who choose one another to work with, and they give each other some feedback. The people who have been in these Practicums have their own Practicums, and meet on their own, or are able to pick up with one another in the community. You can just say, *"Hey, I've got this dream I want to work on...or...this issue going on in my life. Will you sit with me?"* People can even do Gestalt sitting at the bar! Ordinarily, in a situation like that, a person might say something like, *"My wife left me for so and so."* In Gestalt practice, you could use a bottle of beer on the bar, and say, *"O.K. There's your wife. Talk to your wife."* ...And then do a dialogue. You can approach it in this way, rather than as a great-big serious discipline. You look at it as a form of play. In order to do Gestalt with one another, I think all that is required of people is a little experience and the willingness to play.

How much training or skill you really need to be a good reflector is an open question. We have massage at Esalen, as well as other things that require more training, like Rolfing. I consider Gestalt more like massage. You can give a massage that feels good with very little training and very little experience. Some people just have a great aptitude to do massage. On the other hand, some people can train forever, and they never really become good masseuses or masseurs. There is value in training. But Gestalt is an approach that you can do at almost any level. You can do it almost as a game. Workshops are not so much "training." Along with a particular type of aptitude, the more experience you have doing work is more important than any kind of training. Effectively, Fritz didn't train in the usual sense – by supervising carefully. You just hung out with him. For me, learning Gestalt is like that – you hang out with a master of Gestalt and pick it up, and then, like Fritz did with me, you say, *"Dick (or whoever), it's time to go out and teach."* I'd never say that Fritz carefully trained me, with this unit and that unit of knowledge, like in college. The model is much more like the way you would learn something like weaving, or any folk skill, or sculpture, or art. Gestalt Practice is relational – in relationship to your own particular aptitudes and interests. Of course, I have to say that it has made a big difference for me to be able to do Gestalt a lot!

For me, most training in this particular area is false-training – as in social work, in psychiatry, and certainly in psychology. As I said at the beginning, I have an undergraduate degree in psychology from Stanford, and did graduate work at Harvard. It was mis-training. It was an attempt to put people in cognitive boxes, with a lot of denial of the stuff of life – which is basically sensation and feeling.

With respect to this question of training or non-training, I want to say something more about the kind of aptitude a person needs in order to be a reflector. First or all, I think there's a certain personality style that naturally finds our particular approach more comfortable from the point of view of the initiator – the person working. This is quite different from what I think used to be the case with process work in the past, with what I call the "hunger for encounter." That was the attitude of, "Let's make something happen!" In other words, the pattern some people fell into was, "What's the next exciting event I can move to?" Much of the popularity of the encounter movement – and also, I think, the reason for its early demise – was a product of an approach like, "O.K., turn me on, excite me." – "Let's go for a weekend and really turn on." One valid criticism of Esalen is, rather than becoming something of real ongoing value, it has become something that is just an exciting hit, like going to see an Arnold Schwarzenegger movie. For a good reflector there's more of the quality – a certain willingness – to come off that particular excitement-seeking mode, and allow excitement to become something that either happens or doesn't happen – not something that has to happen. I think you need a certain type of patience as a reflector – to recognize and appreciate that particular frame of mind.

So who would make a good reflector? And who wouldn't? That's a little hard to say, because, for me, primarily what Gestalt Practice is about isn't therapy, and it isn't even about personal change. It offers a model for a person to be with himself or herself, and a pattern for two people to be present with one another. It is certainly true that some people seem to simply fall into it. My sense is that anyone who enters their own work successfully can also quite easily shift and take the reflector role as well as the initiator role. When you understand it in your self, and when it has intrinsic value for your self, then you can come from either position. You can look at it as a joint practice, as something done together rather than something that's done by an authority. It takes acceptance – a lot of acceptance, and a lack of the fear of process. In contrast, I can think of some things that really don't work for a reflector – like a lack of detachment, or an investment in where the other person goes and what they should explore.

The basic attitude of a good reflector is the mind-set of being non-judgmental. Being non-judgmental is really a state of mind. Let me give you an example.... You can contact the sense of your fingers touching your face. You can just contact that. You also can judge it – like saying, "I shouldn't be touching my face," or, "I should be rubbing it harder." But can you just be present with that experience? Can you just be present with what you are doing or what your experience is, without putting it into categories that define a judgment? In some ways that can be hard to do.

There is a distinction between criticism and judgment. You can use the word 'criticism' in the sense of being able to discriminate. It is important to be able to discriminate. And to be present with non-judgment doesn't make an appropriate judgment wrong. Some evaluations, some judgments, are right – they're functional. You can sort things out through your own experience, and then you can come to a discrimination, where your judgment is totally appropriate. You determine when that judgment is appropriate from your own experience.

There are probably some appropriate judgments in every relationship, but you can also come to relationship from a non-judgmental context. Let's use an example from work. You may have worked on self-criticism and criticism of others. If you discover that part of your critical-ness is a product of an earlier relationship, hopefully you can resolve that relationship, and then your criticisms won't have what I call "overcharge." For example, person X might do something that makes you angry, and it might appropriately make you angry. But just how angry is it appropriate for you to get? If you have all sorts of un-discharged anger held in back of that, then when something makes you a little angry, it might be the cause for you to explode in anger. Or you might get extremely critical, instead of appropriately critical.

There are some things that are appropriate to be more critical of than others. So, hopefully, coming into contact with you own process, you arrive at a better position of discrimination, where you won't be overcharged. This doesn't mean that you can't criticize. But it does mean that you criticize in a way that's more and more appropriate to self-regulation or the health of the whole. That's my standard for criticism – whether or not it's appropriate to regulation of the whole. For example – consider something that is bad for the environment. It's not a good thing for an industry to dump toxic waste into an open dump. So there, I do have a judgment in an area that I will definitely express. However, hopefully, in the process of expressing that judgment I don't include some un-worked-on rage towards my father or my mother.

So you can put yourself into the Gestalt frame of mind, which is a step back from judgment. Then you can come out of that, into judgment, which is to make a "you should" statement. But then it is important to recognize that you are in a different frame of mind. For instance, let's say you've been beating up on your significant other. In the Gestalt frame, I can come into a reflective position and give you a chance to look at that. I can come into a position where I simply reflect, simply mirror. And I can come out of that into another position, and go over into judgment - and this would be Dick-in-judgment, saying, *"You shouldn't be beating up on your significant other."* But I can also come back to this other position. There is a value in being able to very clearly go to either of these frameworks. Of course, this gets more difficult, the more you get into extreme suffering. There are some issues when it's hard to just be in the reflective position, with things like the Jews in Germany and the death camps. But there's still the possibility to work with the worst atrocity. Ideally, you can come into this framework – even though it gets harder and harder depending upon the issues.

For me, issues of coercion and violence are very hard to be with, in that simple reflective position. I'd like to be able to think that I could work with some of the worst atrocities, in the reflective position. I may or may not be able to do that, if the worst situation were to present itself. Nonetheless, I can also be Dick over here in the non-reflective position. I have that option.

And occasionally in a session I might say something like, *"Hey, this is where I'm coming from. I'm having a hard time staying in my reflective position. So let me shift over here, and now I'm talking as non-reflective Dick."* But I'd say that being able to sit in a non-judgmental Gestalt framework, as much as possible, is one of the most important qualities I would look for in any good reflector.

Looking back over these twenty-four years at Esalen, the one experience that has been the most satisfying is my relationship to my lovely wife, both as a friend and as a fellow practitioner. I met Christine here at Esalen in 1971 when she came to one of my workshops, and we got married in 1974. She became my main collaborator as we developed our brand of Gestalt. As for what I think is most of value to our practice – it is what I do and what Chris does – namely, it is the open way we do Gestalt Practice. What I have seen with some Gestaltists is that, rather than to allow emotion, they try to suppress emotion on the authority of some concept like "that's too dangerous" or "that's bad for you," instead of simply being with what's emerging, and allowing that to happen. In other words, I see that kind of approach, from whatever theoretical framework, as an attempt by some external authority to define what is good for you, instead of being with and trusting process, which is what Chris and I try to do. Other than that, as far as my role in teaching Gestalt at Esalen over the years, I've passed it mostly on to my wife Christine, who I expect to do all the teaching sooner or later.

For the time being, as long as I still teach the practice, there is an expression that I try to remember that goes, "Stinking of Zen." It's used for the kind of person who is so involved in Buddhist practice that their cushion has to be just right, and they have to meditate exactly 45 minutes a night, and not a minute less. In the same way, it's possible to "Stink of Gestalt." So it's important for me to be both in and out of it, and not make a crusade out of it. The truth is, Gestalt is not a cure. It's a practice, and that makes a big difference. A lot of these techniques are presented as though to say, "This is the answer." And I don't feel like Gestalt is the answer. This is a way. It's one way. And it will either be a way that appeals to you, that touches you, that feels familiar to you - or it won't!

Otherwise, I think I've done quite enough talking for one morning. So let's all go down to the Lodge and have lunch. Then after lunch we can come back to this meeting room and begin working together as an open seat group.

Editor's Endnote: Dick Price practiced Gestalt at Esalen until his accidental death on November 25, 1985, when he was struck by a falling boulder while hiking. Besides the difficult work of managing the daily business of Esalen Institute, Gestalt Practice was Dick's most important and lasting achievement.

Dick frequently hiked the trails in the Santa Lucia Mountains behind Esalen for pleasure and for relief from the pressures of running Esalen. Hiking became part of his practice – or what Gary Snyder called "the practice of the wild." It was a solitary practice for Dick, although he often took others along. Sometimes Dick worked with other people while hiking, doing Gestalt Practice sessions along the trail.

Steven Harper was one of Dick's close friends and hiking partners. Steve became a seasoned Gestalt practitioner, a wilderness group leader, and a permanent resident of Big Sur. After Dick's death, Steve was able to have two geographic features officially named for Dick Price. A prominent ridge behind Esalen is now named Price Ridge, and a trail is named Price-Gagarin Trail after Dick and his friend Andrew Gagarin.

In the time since Dick's death, his work has remained influential. Christine Stewart Price, who was Dick's second wife and his principal collaborator in Gestalt work, went on to develop Gestalt Awareness Practice based upon their work together. Dorothy Charles, who was one of Dick's primary students, developed Relational Gestalt Practice. – Dick permanently influenced many lives with his work in Gestalt Practice groups.

In 2013, Christine Price, along with Dorothy Charles, founded an organization named Tribal Ground in Aptos, California, to preserve and grow Dick's practice into the future.

"Trust process, support process,
and get out of the way."
--Dick Price

www.ingramcontent.com/pod-product-compliance
Lightning Source LLC
Chambersburg PA
CBHW021243280526
45784CB00005B/2214